A GIRL LIKE YOU
British Edition

Beth Mullins is nearly 9 years old and she has an embarrassing problem. She doesn't always know when she needs to go to the toilet and sometimes dirties her pants. Her doctor says she has encopresis, but she calls it Sneaky Poo.

At home her Mum and Dad have to tell her when she needs to change her pants, and her best friend Ryan tells her when she has an accident at school. With his help she has managed to keep her problem a secret from everyone else in her class. Until the day when she messes herself in assembly and the girl sitting next to her smells what she has done...

Also available:
A BOY LIKE YOU

For children aged 5 to 8
who withhold their poo
and soil their pants:
HELP! I POO MY PANTS – FOR GIRLS
HELP! I POO MY PANTS – FOR BOYS

A GIRL LIKE YOU
British Edition

James Parkin

www.bigredsock.com

First published under the title *A Child Like You* in 2014

Republished, with amendments and additional material, as *A Girl Like You* in 2016

New edition published 2020

Copyright © James Parkin 2016

The right of James Parkin to be identified as the Author of this Work has been asserted by him in accordance with the Copyright, Designs and Patents Act 1988.

All rights reserved. No part of this publication may be reproduced, stored in a retrieval system, or transmitted in any form or by any means electronic, mechanical, photocopying, recording or otherwise, without the prior permission of the copyright owner.

All characters in this publication are fictitious and any resemblance to real persons, living or dead, is purely coincidental.

Images on the covers and inside pages of this book are copyright and used under licence. All photographs are posed by models.

This book is dedicated to all the children and young people in the world who have soiling problems, and to their parents and carers.

*And also to the memory of
HEATHER LEIGH AYERS
(1988-2014)
a brave girl who battled to overcome encopresis, but was bullied for frequently soiling her pants at school.
RIP*

ACKNOWLEDGEMENTS

A big thank you to all the parents who have commented on my books for children who soil, saying that they had helped them to understand more about the condition and begin a conversation with their son or daughter about their soiling problems, and particularly to those who told me that my books had encouraged their child to try to poo on the toilet.

Many thanks to the wonderful staff and volunteers at ERIC for their support for this project, and for all they do to help children and their families deal with continence issues.

Grateful thanks to Jessica Bukowinski and Michelle Riley for their assistance with the American Edition of the original version of this book, and for their encouragement and support.

Thank you to my friend Dimity Telfer for encouraging me to write more widely about my childhood soiling, and for her own efforts to spread awareness of encopresis.

A big thank you to my wonderful mother, not least for all the times during my childhood when she cleaned me up after I had pooed myself. Sorry for all the dirty pants, Mum!

AND...

To every child who has refused to tease another kid who has wee'd or pooed their pants...

To every parent who has done everything they can think of to help their child overcome their soiling problems...

To every adult who has consoled and helped someone else's child who has toilet issues...

To every member of the medical profession who helps children and young people to overcome continence issues...

To every member of nursery and school staff who has changed children who are past potty training age after they have wet or soiled themselves...

THANK YOU

CONTENTS

1	My Day Out with the Lions	11
2	Beth's Secret	15
3	'Have You Pooed Your Pants Again?'	22
4	Uncle Neil to the Rescue!	32
5	Accident in Assembly	43
6	This is Not Really a Chapter	54
7	Best Friend Forever	59
8	The Surprising Visitor	71
9	A Lesson Learned	78
10	'Happy Birthday, Beth!'	85
	About the Author	91
	Facebook	94
	ERIC – The Children's Bowel and Bladder Charity	99

Chapter One
MY DAY OUT WITH THE LIONS

I stand at the front of the class and look at my homework. Miss Robbins had asked us to write about a happy day in the past. Dale has just read out his piece of writing about going to a football match on his seventh birthday and getting a player's autograph. Now it is my turn.

'My Day Out with the Lions by Beth Mullins,' I begin. I make sure that everyone is listening and no-one is talking before I go on. 'One day my Dad took me and my little brother Jack to Manor Park. I was 5 and there were lions there in big cages that day. The park had brought them over from Africa. Mum didn't come because she wanted to visit a friend. The lions were really big and scary, but I wasn't frightened. One of them roared really loudly and a little boy started crying, but I didn't.'

'Bet she did,' says Carrie to the girl sitting next to her.

'Carrie Johnson,' says Miss Robbins in a stern voice, 'the class did not talk while you told us how you had orange squash and jam sandwiches with the Prime Minister when he came to your eighth birthday party. I ask that you show Beth the same courtesy. Please go on, Beth.'

I start reading again. 'A woman told us about lions. She told us that the boy lions had manes and the girl lions didn't. She also told us how some live in groups called prides and some don't. Dad also bought me and Jack an ice-cream each. And I was happy.'

I lower my piece of paper to show that I had finished.

'Thank you, Beth,' says Miss Robbins, 'it sounds like you had a lovely day. How exciting to see real lions. Thank you for telling us all about it. Now, I think we'll have Nina next, please.'

I walk back to my seat and sit down next to Ryan, who smiles at me. He knows the truth about that horrible day, but nobody else in the classroom does. As Nina begins telling us about the day when she was a bridesmaid, I think about my piece of writing. I had not finished it. I would never finish it because I could not tell the other children in my class what had happened after I'd eaten my ice-cream. I couldn't write down what I'd done before we left the park to go home. The other girls and boys wouldn't find out what had happened that had made my Dad cross, had made my brother laugh and had made me cry.

A girl like me

Actually, it IS me!

Chapter Two
BETH'S SECRET

Ryan leans across and whispers in my ear. Straight away I put my left hand up. If I put my right hand up, it means that I want to ask the teacher something or answer a question. When I put my left hand up, it means that I need to leave the classroom.

Miss Robbins spots my hand. 'All right, run along, Beth.'

The desk that I sit at is at the front of the classroom so I don't have to walk past all the other children when I have to leave the room quickly. I take my schoolbag with me because I'm going to need it. 'Run along' is just a phrase, of course, I'm not allowed to run inside the school. But I do walk quite fast down the corridor because, thanks to Ryan, I know that I smell.

I push open the door of the staff toilets and head towards the last stall. I like to be as far from the sinks as I can be, just in case someone else comes in. When I'm inside the stall I sometimes sit down for a minute and wonder why I have this awful problem. It just seems so unfair, and it's worse when it happens at school. But it's no good feeling sorry for myself. I've got to deal with what I've done and then go back to my class. I reach inside my bag and pull out the things that I need.

Now I don't want to be rude to you, but what I need to do now is really, really private, so you'll have to leave. But I'll see you again in the library at playtime. And if I can find a quiet spot where no-one else can hear, I'll tell you all about my problem. But you must keep it a secret. You must promise not to tell anyone else. Okay?

Well, this is the school library. As you can see, there are lots of books and computers. I've managed to find a quiet corner where I can tell you about my problem. Only one of my classmates knows about it. I wish I could tell everyone else. If I thought they'd all understand that I can't help doing what I do, then I'd tell them. But I'm sure some of them would laugh at me, so I keep it a secret. But I hope you won't laugh at me.

Okay, here goes. I sometimes poo in my pants. There, I've said it. I'll be 9 years old on Saturday and I still dirty my pants sometimes, like a little girl who is 2 or 3 years old and has just stopped wearing nappies.

I know, I know, it's a pretty horrible thing to do. But I can't help it, really I can't. I've got something wrong with my body. I don't know sometimes when I need to go to the toilet. So I just poo my pants without knowing that I'm doing it.

I don't know when I've done it either. I can't smell it or feel it. Someone has to tell me when I need to change my pants. At home Mum or Dad will say something like, 'Beth dear, I think you've had an accident,' which means they can smell that I've pooed myself.

When I'm at school Ryan tells me if I start to smell. He's my best friend and we always sit together. He whispers in my ear that I need to change before anyone else smells what I've done. Then I go to the staff toilets to change my pants. Ryan is the only kid in the school who knows about my problem.

He's never teased me about it and I know he'll never tell anyone else. I wish there were more boys around like Ryan.

I carry a few pairs of spare pants in my schoolbag in case I have an accident in class. I also have a small packet of baby wipes, which I use to clean my bum. And Mum bought me a special little bag to put my dirty pants and the dirty wipes in. The special bag keeps the mess and the smell away from my other things. I can then hide it at the bottom of my schoolbag.

When I first started at this school, Ryan used to come with me to the staff toilets and waited by the sinks while I cleaned myself up. Occasionally I couldn't cope on my own, so I called for Ryan to fetch Mrs Edmonds to help me. Mrs Edmonds often changes the younger children who wet or dirty their pants in class, and she told my Mum and Dad she would be happy to help me if I needed it. I really like her.

There was also one time when I found that I had run out of clean pants, so Ryan had to go to the office to borrow a pair from the school. Luckily, no-one saw him walking down the corridor carrying a pair of girls' pants!

These days I don't have really bad accidents. And before I come to school I always make sure I have spare pants in my schoolbag.

If anyone else in the class asks why I have to leave the room I tell them I have to take special medicine. I don't like lying, but I can't tell them the truth.

My doctor has a special name for what's wrong with me. It's a hard word which I can't remember. I'm going to look it up in the dictionary. That's why I wanted to meet you in the library. Let me just look under the letter E.

Here we are, 'Encopresis', that's what he calls it. Miss Robbins calls it 'Soiling'. I call it 'Sneaky Poo' because my poo sometimes sneaks out of my bottom into my pants.

So now you know my secret, I hope we can be friends. I hope you don't think I'm just a big, smelly baby who's too lazy to go to the toilet. I'm not, really I'm not. I'm not a horrible monster either, I'm just a girl.

A girl like you.

Do you try to avoid using the toilet?

> I didn't go to the toilet and now I've pooed my pants.

> I couldn't hold it in any longer.

Don't try to hold it in!
It wants to come out!

Do you try to hold in your poo?

> I didn't go to the toilet and now I've wet my pants.

> The poo I held inside my body pressed on my bladder and made me wee myself.

Go to the toilet!
Let it go!

Chapter Three
'HAVE YOU POOED YOUR PANTS AGAIN?'

School's out and me and Ryan...sorry, I mean Ryan and I...walk over to where our Mums are waiting for us. My Mum has already picked up Jack, who is standing next to her. When he sees me he sticks his tongue out. Ryan hasn't got any brothers or sisters, lucky thing.

'Did you have a nice day?' Mum asks me. She always asks the same question when I come out of school.

'Great,' I reply. 'We had a Maths test and I came second.'

'Well done, my clever daughter.'

I've always been good at Maths. One day I'll beat Hiren and come top. I lower my voice. 'I had an accident this morning.'

'Were you able to cope all right?'

I nod. 'Ryan told me and I went straight

to the staff toilets.' I smile at Ryan but he isn't looking at me. He's busy telling his Mum about a model he's making in class.

Jack has heard what I've said. 'Smelly girly!' he calls out.

'Jack!' says Mum, 'what have I told you about that? You're not to tease Beth. You know she can't help it.'

He's been calling me 'smelly girly' for years, usually when Mum and Dad aren't around. I find it best to ignore him so he gets fed up of it. Anyway, his toilet habits are not perfect. Last year he nearly wet himself at the local football team's KidzFunDay. I saw that he was fidgeting a lot and had to rush him to the toilets because he said he couldn't wait while I fetched Dad. When Mum used to bath us together he would always wee in the water and think it was funny. (Well, not always but whenever he could, he never used the toilet before he got in the bath!) And once he drank a whole big bottle of pop just before bedtime so, of course, he wet his bed. Then he had to sleep with me for the rest of the night and he wet my bed too. Brothers, who needs them?

Looking at me again, Mum says, 'Rinse out your pants when we get home, Beth, and put them in with the washing.'

'Okay.'

Mum and Dad never tell me off when I have an accident. They know that I don't do it on purpose. Things were different when I first got Sneaky Poo when I was 5.

At first Mum didn't mind too much when I pooed myself. 'Try to remember to use the toilet next time,' she'd say. But when I kept having accidents she began to get cross with me.

'Have you pooed your pants again?' she'd ask me when she could smell what I'd done. It was the sort of question I soon came to dread. I'd say 'no' but then she'd look in my pants and find they were messy. 'Yes, you have. I can't believe you've done this again, and lied about it as well. I'm really ashamed of you, Bethan Lois Mullins.' Then she would take me upstairs to the bathroom to change my pants.

While she was cleaning me up, she'd tell me that I was lazy and naughty. Or that I wasn't a big girl because big girls always used the toilet. Or that if I didn't stop doing it she was going to put me back in nappies.

I'd say I was sorry, but Mum said saying sorry didn't mean anything if I carried on doing it. And she didn't believe me when I told her I didn't know that I'd needed a poo. Once she told me to stand in the corner for ten minutes and think about what I'd done. I stood there facing the wall, feeling miserable, wondering how my clean pants had suddenly become dirty.

Sometimes I went to the toilet for a wee and found that I'd had another accident. I was scared I was going to get shouted at again, so I would take my pants off and hide them in my cupboard or under my bed. But Mum always found them because they made my bedroom smell and then she'd tell me off even more. Other times I'd pull my pants back up again after I'd finished weeing and carry on wearing them, even though they were messy. I hoped that by ignoring my dirty pants they would go away, but they never did.

Dad was really angry with me when I smelled bad while we were watching the lions. 'Beth, you stink!' he said in a loud voice. 'You haven't done it again, have you?' It was only two days after he'd had to change me at Sainsburys. He'd told me then that he'd never have taken me out shopping if he'd known I was going to do that. Of course, I hadn't known I was going to do it either.

He lifted up my dress and checked my pants. I felt like everyone in the park was looking at me. 'Oh you have, you filthy child, you've messed yourself again. You promised to tell me if you needed the toilet.' I looked down at the grass. I didn't want to see the other children staring at me. And I couldn't look at my Dad. I knew that I had broken my promise, but I hadn't meant to. I never pooed myself on purpose. Why would I want to be messy and smelly in the middle of the park? Or in a shop? Or, worst of all, at school?

Dad spoke to my brother. 'I'm sorry, Jack, we're going to have to leave the lions now so I can deal with your naughty sister who has messed her pants again.' By now I was crying. I was still crying when we reached the park toilets.

'I can't take you anywhere, Beth,' said Dad, who had his cross face on. I was holding up my dress while he changed me. Jack was watching because Dad couldn't leave him outside on his own. 'Why didn't you tell me you wanted to go to the toilet, like you promised you would?'

I tried to tell him that I didn't know that I had needed a poo, but I couldn't say anything. It's really hard to talk when you're crying.

'You should be ashamed of yourself, doing this at your age,' Dad went on. 'Your brother doesn't poo himself and he's only 3.'

Jack was finding it very funny that his big sister needed her pants changing.

'I'm not surprised he's laughing at you,' said Dad, as he put my lovely *Frozen* pants in a bag and threw them in the bin. 'All the other children will laugh at you if you keep messing yourself like a baby.'

I just stood there crying my eyes out. I was still crying when we left the park. I felt really miserable. My lovely day out with the lions had been ruined. And all because my stupid body hadn't told me to go to the toilet.

And then there were those days when I needed changing two or three times and Mum got really, really cross. 'It's less than an hour since I put these pants on you and you've pooed them already,' she said sharply as she changed me in the toilets at the public library. 'Just look at the state of them, I don't know why I bother to buy you nice underwear. Why do you keep doing this,

Beth?' I didn't know how to answer so I didn't say anything. I didn't know why it happened, why I couldn't keep my pants clean.

Mum went on, 'This is the third time today you've pooed your pants. What on earth's the matter with you? Do you think I enjoy cleaning up a pooey 5 year old all the time? Do you think I've got nothing better to do? I hate taking you out, Beth. I want us to have a nice time when we go out, not spend half the day changing your pants and cleaning your bottom. For pity's sake, just go to the toilet when you need to. You're a big girl now, start behaving like one.'

At my old school the children used to tease me sometimes. They called me 'pooey pants', 'smelly bum' or 'nappy girl'. They didn't do it all the time, but I still hated it. One boy always pinched his nose when I walked past him, even though I was usually clean.

Miss Peters, the teaching assistant, also got tired of having to take me out of the classroom to change me. 'Beth, if you need to poo don't just do it in your pants,' she'd say to me. 'Ask to go to the toilet, like all the other children do.' If only I could.

Instead I had to stand bare bummed in the girls toilets, praying no-one else would come in and see me being changed. Had to watch my dirty pants being put in a see-through bag to be handed to my Mum at going home time. And, as I got nearer to my 6th birthday, I had to listen to Miss Peters say things like, 'You're far too old to be having accidents like this all the time. It's not fair on the rest of the class. I can't help the other children with their work if I'm in here with you, dealing with this mess. And it's not fair on me. How would you like to have to clean up a nearly 6 year old girl after she's pooed herself? You are being very lazy and selfish, Beth. You're not a baby. Girls of your age do not mess their pants, they go to the toilet.'

I'd promise her that I would always use the toilet from now on. I really, really wanted to be like my classmates. Then the next day, or the day after, or the day after the day after, I'd poo myself again.

In the end Mrs Armitage, my teacher, told my Mum she would have to send me to school in pull-ups. Now I really did feel like 'nappy girl', although it wasn't too bad when I got used to it. Mum didn't like me wearing pull-ups as she thought I would wee in them on purpose, but I didn't. We were both pleased when my new school said I could wear normal pants. The worst thing about being in a pull-up was when we got changed for PE and all the class saw it.

By the time I was 6 I was really fed up. Fed up of dirty pants. Fed up of being the only 6 year old in the whole world who still pooed herself, or so I thought. Fed up of being changed like a toddler, at home, at school and anywhere I went. Fed up of all the tummy aches I got. Fed up of being told off. Fed up of being shouted at. Fed up of my brother calling me 'smelly girly'. Fed up of being teased at school. Fed up of hearing Miss Peters tell my Mum that I had once again failed to use the school toilets and messed my pants or my pull-up. Fed up of everything.

And then everything changed.

Are you drinking enough?

> When I go to the toilet, my wee is dark yellow.

> You're not drinking enough. Your wee should be light yellow, almost like water.

> Drink 6 - 8 glasses of water, squash or juice every day.

> This will help your bladder to fill and stretch so it can hold more wee and stay healthy. It will also help your poo to keep moving!

What colour is YOUR wee?

Chapter Four
UNCLE NEIL TO THE RESCUE!

One afternoon my Uncle Neil came round to babysit me. It was a week after my sixth birthday. My usual babysitter had said she wouldn't be coming round anymore. Mum told me it was because the poor girl was sick of washing my pooey bottom. Mum and Dad were taking Jack to see a film that afternoon. Dad said I couldn't go to the cinema until I stopped dirtying my pants. I also wasn't allowed to go to birthday parties because I might need changing. I'd already been told I couldn't go to my cousin Emily's party.

Mum and Dad didn't tell Uncle Neil about my accidents. They thought he wouldn't want to look after me if he knew that he may have to change me out of messy pants. Mum was also trying to keep my problem a secret as much as she could. She said to me, 'I don't want other members of my family knowing about your babyish and disgusting habit, so you'd better not do it today, young lady. If you do then your uncle will be very cross with you. He certainly won't expect a girl of your age to use her pants as a toilet.'

I liked Uncle Neil a lot. He always played with me and Jack when he came round. I think he liked playing with us because he wasn't married and didn't have any children of his own to play with. He often gave me piggy backs or let me sit on his shoulders. And he always brought sweets for us. I had never seen him be angry with anyone. But maybe he would be cross if he had to deal with a pooey and smelly 6 year old girl. I hoped that I didn't have an accident while he was babysitting me. But I did.

I was painting a picture when it happened. Uncle Neil asked, 'What's that smell? Have you farted, Beth?'

I knew I hadn't, but I nodded. I guessed that I'd pooed.

'I don't know what you've been eating, Beth,' Uncle Neil went on, 'but that was one smelly fart!'

I giggled, but at the same time I was scared. I carried on painting and hoped that the smell would go away.

The smell didn't go away. Five minutes later Uncle Neil asked, 'Beth, what *is* that smell? Do you need to go to the toilet?'

I stopped painting and looked at the carpet. 'I think I've already pooed.'

Uncle Neil stared at me. 'Already pooed? Where?'

'In my pants.' I couldn't look at him. I felt so, oh, what is that long word? Hang on, let me get the dictionary again. It's another E word. Embarrassed. That's it, I felt embarrassed. It was horrible knowing that I'd pooed my pants in front of my uncle, and then having to tell him that I'd done it.

Uncle Neil carried on staring at me for what seemed like a long time. Then he said, 'Come here, Beth.'

I walked over to him, looking at my shoes. I knew I was about to be told off.

He turned me around and sniffed at my trousers. 'Yes, I think you have done something. Oh dear, I suppose I'd better change you. Or would you rather do it yourself?'

I'd never changed myself and I didn't like the idea much. I looked up at him with eyes that were about to cry. 'Will you change me?' It was another embarrassing moment, having to ask my uncle to change my pants.

'All right. Let's go up to the bathroom and sort you out. But I warn you, I'm not used to dealing with pooey kids. I've never even changed a dirty nappy. I'll probably get poo everywhere.'

He reached out his hand and I took it. As we got nearer to the bathroom I began to get really worried. I hadn't pooed in the toilet today or yesterday, so I guessed that my pants and my bum would be really messy. Oh, why did this have to happen now? I wondered if Uncle Neil would shout at me when he pulled down my pants and found out how pooey I was, or just tell me off. He might even smack me.

But my uncle wasn't really cross with me. He was just surprised that I'd done it. 'I can't believe you've gone in your pants at your age,' he said as he did his best to clean me up. 'Don't you think you're a bit too old to be doing this, Beth?'

'I'm sorry,' I said, still trying not to cry, 'I didn't mean to.'

'Why didn't you go to the toilet?' he asked.

'I didn't know I needed to go.'

Uncle Neil didn't say 'Don't talk rubbish' like Mum and Dad did. Instead he said, 'You poor thing. Okay, that's got the worst off. Let's get you into the bath and make you really clean again.'

When Mum and Dad came home Uncle Neil told them what I'd done. Mum said I did it all the time because I couldn't be bothered to go to the toilet, but Uncle Neil said I might have something wrong with my body. He thought they should take me to see the doctor. So the next day that's what Mum did.

I hated sitting in front of the doctor while Mum told him that I still dirtied my pants. 'She just won't go to the toilet when she needs to open her bowel,' Mum told him, 'and just does it in her pants instead, wherever she happens to be. She even did it in church last Sunday. And then she comes out with some rubbish about not knowing she needed to go, and she denies that she's soiled her pants when I can smell that she has.' I stared at my shoes and pretended that she was talking about another little girl who made nasty messes in her underwear.

The doctor, however, was really nice. He told me and Mum that a lot of children have problems using the toilet.

'You mean other children poo themselves?' asked Mum. 'Even at Beth's age?'

'Many other girls and boys have soiling problems, Mrs Mullins,' the doctor replied, 'and some of them are a lot older than your daughter. Even some teenagers and young adults have this condition.'

'So Beth isn't just being lazy?'

'No,' said the doctor, 'she's probably telling the truth about not knowing when she needs a poo. She probably also doesn't know when she's done it.' He looked at me. 'Beth, do you know when you're pooing in your pants? Can you feel yourself doing it?'

I shook my head.

'And do you know afterwards that your underwear is dirty?'

I shook my head again. 'I don't know until Mummy tells me I smell. Then she looks in my pants. Or Daddy does.'

The doctor nodded and looked at my Mum. 'Mrs Mullins, your daughter has encopresis.'

When we got home Mum gave me a big hug. 'I'm so sorry, Beth,' she said. 'I'm sorry I told you off and shouted at you. I'm sorry that I didn't believe you when you told me you didn't know when you needed to poo. I didn't realise you were poorly. But now Daddy and I will help you to get better.'

She kissed the top of my head. I hugged her tightly. I'd thought I was the only 6 year old in the world who pooed her pants. But I wasn't. Lots of other kids had the same problem as me. And now Mum and Dad were going to help me and be nice to me.

'No more shouting at you or telling you off,' said Mum. 'I won't let Jack laugh at you or tease you. You can go to your cousin Emily's birthday party next week. We'll take some spare pants along and I'll change you if you have an accident. And we'll all work together to help you to use the toilet and keep your pants clean. Would you like that, Beth?'

Of course I would. I wanted it more than anything else in the world.

'And no more hiding your pants,' Mum told me. 'If you find your pants are dirty just tell me or Daddy and we won't be cross with you. All right?'

I promised that I would never hide my pants again. And I kept this promise.

From then on I didn't get told off or

shouted at when I had an accident. If I started to smell on a day out then Mum or Dad took me to the toilets, or behind a wall or a big tree if we were outdoors, and checked my pants. If I had pooed they just changed me without any fuss and we carried on having a good time. Even when I did it in the car and Dad had to change my pants in a lay-by, he didn't get cross with me. Uncle Neil also took me out sometimes and he soon became an expert on cleaning up pooey kids!

But when I was at home I still hated it when I pulled down my pants to have a wee and found that I'd pooed in them. I now knew that it wasn't my fault, but I still felt bad about it. And I didn't like telling Mum or Dad or a babysitter that I needed changing. Even though I knew no-one would be cross with me, admitting to anyone that I'd dirtied my pants again was still really embarrassing.

When I was 6 and a half Mum showed me how to change myself after an accident, so I wouldn't need a grown-up to do it. At first I thought cleaning poo off my bum was really yucky and I didn't want to do it. But then I decided that it was great that I could take care of myself. No more having to ask someone else to change me. From now on I was allowed to check my pants myself if someone said I smelled bad, and could clean myself up when I had to.

Being able to change myself also meant that Mum could leave me at birthday parties, and playdates at the home of my friend Vicky didn't finish early because I'd pooed myself.

Vicky's Mum didn't mind that I had accidents but she'd never been willing to change me. Whenever Vicky had said to her, 'Beth has dirty knickers,' or she could smell that I was pooey, she had called my Mum to take me home and that was the end of the playdate.

Okay, that's enough about what happened when I was 5 and 6. Now we're going back to the present time.

Public toilets won't bite your bum!

> Some adults try to avoid doing a poo (or even a wee) in pubic toilets.

> That's nonsense! Don't try to hold on until you get home. Get into good habits while you're still a kid.

Show the grown-ups how it's done!

Germs love unwashed hands!

> Don't forget to wash your hands after using the toilet.

> I always wash my hands when I've been to the loo!

> Whether I've done Number 1 or Number 2!

Chapter Five
ACCIDENT IN ASSEMBLY

Oh, this is not a very good place to start this chapter. I'm just about to do a toilet sit. That's where I sit on the toilet for ten minutes and try to…well, you can probably guess by now! I don't feel like I need to go at the moment. But I'd better try, as I had an accident yesterday and I haven't been today.

When I was 6, I did toilet sits every day. Mum used to sit in front of me and we'd sing songs and play games. She'd praise me for trying and give me a hug if I did anything. It was much better than being told off for having an accident. Mum doesn't sit with me anymore but she still praises me when I use the toilet.

I'd better go now before Jack starts banging on the bathroom door, saying he's bursting for a wee. I'm sure he does it on purpose. I've got a new book from the library to read. Sometimes I borrow Mum's iPad to play with, but today I'm going to read.

Why don't we meet up again at school tomorrow? We've got an assembly in the morning, I'll see you there. Now go away, please, there are some things a girl has to do alone!

Hello again! Welcome to the school assembly. We have one every week, always on Wednesday. Well, not always on Wednesday. Sometimes we have it on another day. When someone off local TV came to talk to us she could only come on a Friday. And we always have a special assembly on Hallowe'en and that could be on any day. But mostly we have assembly on a Wednesday. And it's always straight after playtime. Well, nearly always.

We haven't got a visitor today. Mr Hayling, who teaches Year 6, is talking to us instead. He's telling us all about when he was a boy and how he had to help on the farm where he lived. He's quite old, so they probably had dinosaurs on the farm. It's a bit boring but I try to pay attention. Miss Robbins will probably ask us what assembly was about when we get back to class and I don't want her to think I haven't been listening.

Ryan is sitting next to me, like he always does in the classroom. Just as Mr Hayling is telling us how it was his job to feed the chickens every morning, Ryan whispers in my ear. For a moment I freeze. I've never had an accident in assembly before. There's no point in putting my left hand up as Mr Hayling won't know what it means. Miss Robbins isn't here, she's gone back to the classroom. Nor is Mrs Edmonds. Still unsure what I should do, I carry on sitting here while I make up my mind.

Okay, I've decided to ask another teacher if I can go to the toilet. We're supposed to go at playtime but they usually let you go during assembly if you have to. I stand up and clamber over the other children.

Mrs Bailey is the nearest teacher, so I walk up to her. I don't stand too close to her. I don't want her to smell what I've done in my pants. 'Can I go to the toilet please, Mrs Bailey?'

'Are you sure you can't wait, Beth?' she asks. 'Assembly is nearly over. And you really should have gone at playtime.'

'I did go at playtime,' I tell her, which is true as I had been for a wee.

'Well, your bladder can't have filled up again in that time. You'd better go and sit down again and see if Miss Robbins will let you go to the toilet after assembly. If you went at playtime then there's not much risk of you making a puddle on the floor.'

I don't want to tell her the truth. And I really don't want to sit down in line again knowing how bad I must smell. I decide to lie and tell her I really need to do a poo. When I was younger I didn't like saying in day nursery that I needed to do a poo-poo (as I called it then). Not anymore. These days I don't mind telling an adult that I need a poo.

I open my mouth to speak, but then Mrs Bailey's face changes. She can smell me. She knows that I've pooed my pants. I can tell she's trying not to look disgusted. Her face has the same look that I often saw on the face of Miss Peters at my old school when she was changing my pants or my pull-up. 'All right, Beth, I understand,' Mrs Bailey says. 'You may go to the toilet.' She tries to smile at me.

'Thank you, Mrs Bailey.' I walk towards the door, glad to have escaped at last.

The girls and boys toilets are right outside the Assembly Hall, but I walk past them. I go first to my classroom to get my bag. Miss Robbins is sitting at her desk, marking our Maths work. She looks up as I walk into the room. 'Have you soiled yourself, Beth?' she asks.

I nod. 'Ryan told me that I needed to change. I asked Mrs Bailey if I could go to the toilet. She didn't want to let me go, but then she smelled me and knew that I'd already done it in my pants.'

Miss Robbins smiles. 'Don't worry, Beth, all the teachers know about your soiling problem, they know you can't help having accidents sometimes.'

'They do?'

Miss Robbins nods. 'They have to know, in case they have to teach this class when I'm not here. And they know that no other child is aware of your problem apart from Ryan, and that if you raise your left hand it means you need to leave the room straight away.'

So maybe I could have put up my left hand in assembly after all. I pick up my bag.

'You had better come back here when you're finished,' says Miss Robbins. 'I think assembly will be over by then.'

I head to the staff toilets. They're nearly always empty because teachers aren't allowed to go to the toilet during lessons. Mrs Edmonds uses these toilets to change children who have had accidents, as they're more private than the girls or boys toilets. She also puts a sign that says, 'Do Not Enter' on the door when she does this. Why couldn't my old school have done that when Miss Peters was changing me? It was horrible when other girls came into the toilets and laughed at me.

I saw the sign on the door when I had to change myself a few weeks ago. I knocked on the door and Mrs Edmonds let me come in because she didn't want to leave me in the corridor smelling of poo. 'It's all right, Harry,' she said to the child she was changing, 'Beth won't tell anyone about your little accident.'

'It'll be our little secret, okay?' I said to the Year 1 boy who had wet his pants. I haven't done that since I was 4 and I didn't want to stop playing pass the parcel at Georgia Westwood's birthday party. But my doctor told me and my Mum…I mean, my Mum and me…that some children who have Sneaky Poo also wet themselves sometimes.

This time there's no sign on the door of the staff toilets, so I walk in. There's no-one else here. Okay, so it's off to the end stall to clean myself up once again. See you later!

'Hi, smelly bum!' says a girl's voice.

Oh no! I stop walking across the playground as I hear those awful words. Nobody has ever called me that horrible name at this school. I can't have pooed myself again, can I? Ryan isn't here to tell me, he's playing football with a group of boys. Should I quickly go to the staff toilets to check my pants? No, I won't. It's been ages since I had two accidents on the same day. I really don't think my pants are dirty again. Instead I turn around to see who has called me 'smelly bum.'

It's Carrie Johnson. She was the girl who got told off by Miss Robbins in the first chapter. Do you remember? She said something to her friend while I was reading my homework out loud. 'I see you know your name,' she says as I look at her.

I walk up to her. I don't want everyone in the playground to hear us. 'Why did you call me that?' I ask her.

'Well, I sat next to you in assembly this morning,' she replies, 'and you smelled like my baby sister does when she needs her nappy changing. Only worse.'

I stare at her. I had forgotten that she had been sitting on the other side of me in assembly. I remembered how I'd just sat there for a minute after Ryan had whispered in my ear, wondering what to do.

I'm wondering what to do now, what to say in reply. I'm about to tell her that it's not very nice to compare me to a baby in a dirty nappy. I decide to laugh as I say it, to try to make it sound like a ridiculous idea that I could smell like her little sister. But before I say anything Carrie asks me a question. It's like the questions that I always dreaded when I was 5. 'Had you pooed your knickers?'

'No!' I say at once, in too loud a voice.

Carrie looks taken aback. I don't think she expected me to answer so fiercely. It probably makes it look like I'm lying. Which I am, of course.

'Don't be silly,' I say in a quieter voice.

'Of course I hadn't.'

'Well you did stink,' Carrie says.

An idea comes to me. 'How do know it was me? It could have been someone on the other side of you. Or in front of you. Or behind you.'

Carrie smiles at me, but it's not a nice smile. 'Because it stopped when you got up and went over to Mrs Bailey. So I know it was you.'

I'm getting worried. Was Carrie about to find out my secret? She was a bit of a tell-tale. I couldn't stand it if she told everyone in the class what I did. It would be like my old school all over again. Only it would be worse now because I was three years older. I couldn't bear it if I got teased again because of my toilet problem.

I know I'm going to have to find a way to explain the smell. 'Look, I just farted, all right?'

'So why did you leave assembly?' Carrie wants to know.

'To go to the toilet, of course.'

'Liar! I watched you. You didn't go in the girls toilets. You walked past them.'

Now I really don't know what to say. I just stare at her, trying to think of another reason for leaving assembly. I'll admit to anything now, except the truth.

'And you didn't come back to assembly,' Carrie goes on.

Quick, let me think of something. 'I…I…I…' But I can't think of anything.

'Where did you go? Did you go off to the Nursery? Did you ask Miss Tansey to change your pooey knickers?'

I can't stand it anymore. Carrie is too close to the truth. I turn around and run away from her. At first I don't know where I'm going, then I head for a hiding place behind the storeroom. Me and Ryan…I mean…oh, you know what I mean…sometimes come here when we want to be on our own. I want to be on my own right now.

Okay, I'm here, away from the teachers, away from the other children and, best of all, away from Carrie Johnson. I sit down and put my head in my hands.

What are you doing here? Didn't you hear me, I want to be on my own. Stop following me around, can't you?

Look, go away, leave me alone. How many times do I have to say it?

LEAVE ME ALONE!

Don't sit in your poo!

> Don't carry on wearing messy knickers.

> Change yourself or tell someone that you've had an accident.

> Phew, she stinks! Remember, even if you can't smell your poo, other kids and adults can!

Get changed!
Get clean!

Chapter Six
THIS IS NOT REALLY A CHAPTER

I'm sorry.

I'm really, really sorry.

I didn't mean to be so rude to you after I'd run away from Carrie. I just needed to be on my own for a bit. I couldn't bear the thought of everyone teasing me again if they found out my secret. Some of the class would probably be really mean to me if they discovered that I pooed my pants at my age. And they may tease Ryan too for being best friends with a girl who still can't use the toilet properly. Then he might not want to be my friend anymore. Oh why didn't I leave assembly straight away? Why did I sit there smelling of poo?

Having Sneaky Poo does make me a bit bad tempered sometimes. I get really cross with my body for not telling me when I need the toilet and I snap at people like my Mum or Dad or my brother or even Ryan. It's stupid of me to do it, it's not their fault I have this problem, and I say sorry afterwards. But you don't always think about what you're doing while you're doing it, do you?

When I was 6 and 7 I sometimes refused to change myself when Mum or Dad told me I'd had an accident. I insisted that I was clean and didn't need to change, so I got sent to my bedroom. I just thought that if I didn't look at my dirty pants then I could pretend that they weren't messy and I hadn't pooed myself yet again. So I didn't clean myself up and made my bedroom stink so bad that even I could smell it. But I still carried on playing in dirty pants and tried to ignore the smell. It sounds a pretty horrid thing to do now, but it seemed a good idea at the time.

In the end I always had to change if I wanted to leave my smelly bedroom. Sometimes I didn't change until bedtime. Other times I changed myself because it was time for tea or I wanted to watch the television. Mum wouldn't let me sit at the dinner table or on the sofa if I was stinky and I didn't want to go hungry or miss my favourite programmes.

Mum and Dad no longer told me off for having accidents but they did get cross with me when I wouldn't deal with my messes. Happily, I grew out of this habit. I knew the mess I had made in my pants wasn't going to go away by itself and it was no good pretending that I hadn't pooed myself when I had. Also Mum told me that it was bad for my health to stay in dirty pants. She said I might get something called an infection which would make it hurt when I went to the toilet for a wee.

So I don't do that anymore, but I still sometimes get cross with my body and I take it out on other people. But I'm really sorry I took it out on you. I hope we can still be friends.

This is not really a chapter of the story. It's just me saying sorry.

Can't do a poo? Toot on the loo!

I'm finding it hard to push my poo out of my bum.

Try playing a toy trumpet while you're sitting on the toilet.

He's not joking! We use the same muscles for blowing that we use for pooing!

Running around is also good for getting poo moving. And boys can try sitting down on the toilet to do a wee sometimes. There could also be a poo ready to come out!

Pooed in the toilet? Well done! Now wipe from front to back!

> Hi! This advice is really important for girls, so make sure you always follow it!

> It's so the germs in your poo don't get near where your wee comes out.

It's good advice for boys as well!

Don't be back to front! Wipe FRONT to BACK!

Chapter Seven
BEST FRIEND FOREVER

Hello again. I'm glad we're still friends. I'm going over to play at Ryan's house soon. My Mum's taking me over there, and I'll have my tea there as well. Then Ryan's Mum will walk me home again. I'm glad I'm going to see Ryan tonight. I want to tell him that Carrie is probably going to tell everyone about what I did in assembly.

I'm dreading going to school tomorrow. I'm sure by playtime all the class will know about my accident. Of course, they won't know that I do it a lot or that I've been doing it since I was 5. But even pooing your pants once is bad enough when you're nearly 9. And they may start to guess why I leave the classroom a lot and walk in the opposite direction to the girls toilets. I'm probably going to get teased every day now until I leave big school when I'm 18. I just hope Ryan still wants to be my friend. Please don't let the other boys tease him about hanging around with the girl who smells.

Ryan and I...see, I got it right that time...have been friends since I moved house when I was 6. We moved during the summer holidays. Mum took Jack and me to the local park and Ryan was already playing there. He asked me if I'd help him make sandcastles so we made a really big one in the sandpit. Then we rode on the swings (I went higher), played on the see-saw and went on the climbing frames. I'd never had a boy as a friend but I really liked Ryan. He wasn't silly like my brother and he let me share his sweets. And he didn't get cross with Jack when the little brat ruined our big sandcastle by jumping on it.

We begged our Mums to let us play together again at the park. We went back the next day. Then Ryan's Mum asked if I would like to play with Ryan at his house tomorrow and have lunch there. I said, 'Yes please,' and our Mums sorted everything out. I was now living a long way away from my friend Vicky and I really wanted a new friend.

But the next day I was nervous. By now I was able to change myself and was doing toilet sits every day but I was still having a lot of accidents. What if I pooed myself in front of Ryan? He would probably think I was a baby who still wasn't potty trained and not want to be my friend anymore. Or he might tease me, just like the children at my old school. Vicky hadn't minded because she knew I couldn't help it, but Ryan didn't know that. So, my Mum gave Ryan's Mum a ring before I went over there.

'…I just wanted to tell you that Beth has a problem doing her number 2s,' Mum said over the telephone. 'She doesn't know when she needs to go to the toilet, so most days she soils her pants.'

I walked out of the room and went upstairs. I hated hearing Mum tell other people about my problem. I knew she had to do it, like she had told my aunts and uncles so they didn't think I was being lazy or doing it on purpose if I had an accident in their homes. But I still didn't like hearing her say the words.

Mum came up to my bedroom a few minutes later. She sat next to me on my bed. 'It's all right, Beth,' she said to me, 'Ryan's Mum is going to talk to him before we get there and tell him you have a little problem using the toilet. She's sure that he won't mind if you have an accident. He has a cousin who wets the bed, and occasionally wets herself during the day, and he's never teased her about it. I've also told Ryan's Mum that you don't know when your pants are dirty, so she's going to ask Ryan to tell you if you need to change. Can't have you stinking out his bedroom, can we?'

I shook my head. It would be…that word yet again…embarrassing to have my new friend, who was a boy, tell me that I'd dirtied my pants. But it was better than being messy and smelly for ages and not knowing. And I wouldn't have to tell his Mum that I'd pooed myself and ask her to change me.

I had a great time playing at Ryan's house. During the rest of the summer holidays we played together nearly every day. Sometimes round my house, sometimes at Ryan's house, sometimes at the park. And on some days my Mum or Ryan's Mum took us out for the day. Ryan always told me when I needed to change, but he was never unkind about it. At first he told me out loud. I didn't mind this until the day when he said in SchoolsOut, 'Beth, you've pooed your pants.' Other families nearby turned and stared at me.

After that his Mum said he should just whisper in my ear.

We also had sleepovers sometimes, and still do. My doctor said that some kids with Sneaky Poo have accidents at night, but I've never pooed my pyjamas and I haven't wet the bed since I was really little. Ryan's Mum said it wouldn't matter if I was likely to have accidents as I could wear the bedtime pants that she keeps for Ryan's cousin when she sleeps over, but I didn't need them.

On the Wednesday before I was going to start at my new school, I went to a play scheme at my church, which was in the next town. Ryan came with me because I didn't really know anyone else and I wanted to have a friend with me. During the afternoon he told me that I'd had an accident. At the time I was sitting next to him at the craft table, working on a collage. The table was at the opposite end of the large room to the cloakroom and toilets. I now had to do the 'walk of shame' past all the other children in the room.

I stood up and got a surprise. Ryan stood up as well and took my hand. He whispered that we would go together, then no-one would know which of us was smelly. I whispered back, 'Thank you.'

As we started to walk across the room I got another surprise. Ryan had a sad look on his face, and he began walking in an unusual way. He was pretending that his pants were messy! I knew that he was copying the way I had walked after I had not pooed for three days and then had a really, really bad accident while playing in his garden. (Okay, Ryan's Mum changed me that time, but she was cool with it.)

Some of the children looked at us in a strange way as we went past. I heard one girl say to her friend, 'Look at the way that boy's walking. And he stinks! Bet he's pooed himself!' The two girls both giggled and held their noses. Ryan screwed his face up like he was about to cry. I couldn't believe that he was doing this for me, but I was really grateful. His family doesn't go to church so he probably wouldn't see any of the other children again.

'Great, there's no-one here,' said Ryan when we got to the cloakroom. He suddenly looked happy again.

'That was brilliant!' I said. 'You really fooled those girls by walking like that. Thank you, thank you, thank you!' I almost wanted to hug him, but I couldn't do that while I was still pooey!

I pulled my spare pants out of my coat. Ryan waited for me while I got cleaned up, then we returned to the craft table. But before we went back, I told him he was my best friend forever.

I'm in Ryan's bedroom now. We're playing a new board game, but I'm finding it hard to keep my mind on it. I keep thinking about Carrie and what she will do. I'm starting to think I will tell Mum I'm poorly tomorrow so I don't have to go to school. I'm getting so worried about it, I think I probably *will* be sick anyway. I just hope I get to the toilet in time. I don't want to be sick in my bed or on the floor. Or do it all over the table while I'm having breakfast like Jack once did.

'She's going to tell the whole class,' I say to Ryan while he's rolling the dice. He throws a double 6 and wins the game. 'Everyone's going to know what a baby I am.'

'You're not a baby,' says Ryan. 'You know you can't help having accidents. And nobody ever believes what Carrie says. Remember last term when she told us she went on a day trip to Jupiter? Everyone knew that she was making it up. So even if she tells people about what happened in assembly, they won't think it's true. They'll just think she's being silly.'

I'm not so sure. Going on a visit to another planet was impossible. A girl in Year 4 pooing her pants at school was unlikely, but not impossible. I was certain that at least a few people would believe Carrie. And they wouldn't allow me to forget about it. All the teasing I had had to put up with at my old school was about to start all over again.

'Anyway,' Ryan goes on, 'you don't have many accidents these days, do you?'

'I've had two this week already,' I remind him. 'And both of them at school. I hate it when it happens at school. I'm always afraid someone else will find out. And now someone has.'

Ryan thinks for a moment, then he says, 'I wish you didn't have Sneaky Poo, Beth.'

'Why?' I ask. 'So you wouldn't have a smelly friend?'

'No. I just know that it makes you sad

sometimes. When I grow up I'm going to be a doctor and I'll find a cure for Sneaky Poo.'

'That's nice,' I tell him. 'But I thought you wanted to be a racing driver.'

'Well, I do. But I won't be racing all the time. I'll be a doctor and find a cure in my spare time. And I'll build a special hospital that only helps kids with Sneaky Poo. And they can stay there until they're better. And none of them will be teased because all the boys and girls there have accidents. And the nurses will be really kind and not tell anyone off and make sure everyone has spare pants with pictures on them. And everyone will play together and have a really great time and be really, really good friends.'

'It sounds lovely,' I say. I know Ryan won't really do it, but it's nice to pretend.

I have something important that I want to ask him. 'Ryan, if the others in the class do find out that I have Sneaky Poo, will you still want to be my friend?'

He answers straight away. 'Of course. I'll always want to be your friend.'

I smile. For the first time since I met Carrie in the playground I feel a bit happier. 'Thank you,' I say.

'One young lady safely delivered,' says Ryan's Mum to my Dad as he opens the front door. He thanks her for looking after me and I thank her for having me. I say goodbye to Ryan and then he and his Mum go back to his house.

'Hi Beth, did you have a nice time?' asks my Mum as she walks into the hallway. I nod. I did have a nice time but now my tummy is starting to feel funny. I know it's because I'm worrying about tomorrow again. But then I get the surprise of my life.

'You have a visitor,' Mum tells me. 'She arrived a few minutes ago, her father dropped her off. I said you were due home soon so she decided to wait for you. She's in the sitting room.'

I wonder who on earth it can be and why she has come to see me. I walk into the room. I can see a girl sitting on the sofa. She stands up when she hears me enter and turns to face me. 'Hello, Beth,' she says.

It is Carrie Johnson.

My best friend forever

Ryan

Somewhere new?
Use the loo!

Being willing to use any toilet is an important lifeskill.

Try to use the loo when you go somewhere new!

And you CAN poo at a friend's home! I just have!

You ARE allowed to go Number 2!

Chapter Eight
THE SURPRISING VISITOR

'Did you poo your knickers in assembly?' Carrie asks.

We are in my bedroom, sitting on my bed. I could say 'no'. Carrie still doesn't know for sure that I did it. But I don't think she'd believe me, not after the way I ran off earlier. So I nod my head. 'I couldn't help it,' I say. 'I never can. It just happens.'

Carrie's eyes open wide. 'Do you mean you do it a lot?'

Oh no, now I've really given the game away. I can't even pretend now that it was just a one-off accident. I nod my head a second time. 'I have Sneaky Poo.'

'Sneaky Poo? What's that?' Carrie asks.

So I tell her. I also borrow Mum's iPad and find a website all about it. Carrie has a quick look at it. 'That's awful,' she says.

'I'm really sorry, Beth. I wouldn't have said anything to you in the playground if I'd known you really had done it.'

'You wouldn't?'

'No. When I spoke to you I didn't really think you had pooed yourself. I was only teasing you. I've never heard of someone our age pooing her knickers. I didn't think anyone did it.'

'That's part of the problem,' I tell her. 'Hardly any children have heard of Sneaky Poo so if they found out I pooed myself all the time they'd just think I was being a baby and laugh at me. Even my Mum and Dad thought I was being lazy until Mum took me to see the doctor.'

'Did the doctor help you?'

I nod. 'Oh yes. I'm much better than I used to be. When I was 5 and 6, I was having accidents nearly every day. Sometimes I even had two or three accidents in a day. Now I only have one or two a week. But the best thing was knowing that I wasn't the only kid who had this problem.'

'So a lot of kids have Sneaky Poo?'

'Yes.' I pick up the iPad again and type 'soils pants' into a search engine. Seconds later thousands of results appear. I click on the first one. It's a post on the messageboard of a website for parents. I pass the iPad over to Carrie.

Carrie reads the post out loud. 'My son is 11 years old and keeps messing his pants. He does it anywhere, at home, at school, at friends' homes, in the car, at the cinema, even at the table of a restaurant. Yesterday he came home from Scouts in messy pants. He said he didn't know when it happened and I hate to think how long he might have been sitting in his own waste. This has been going on for years now. I can't understand why he keeps doing this at his age.'

'I can,' I say. 'It's because he has Sneaky Poo.'

Carrie reads the first reply. 'I thought I was the only mother who had a child who did this! My daughter is 12 and she is just the same as your son. When we go out I plead with her to use the toilet but she just soils herself wherever she is. She doesn't even care that she's done it. She says she knows when she's messy but she'd walk around in soiled knickers for hours if I let her. I feel like I've failed as a parent when I'm out in public with a 12 year old girl who smells like a sewer, but it doesn't seem to bother her.

I'm guessing that she's messed her knickers so many times over the years that she thinks it's normal to be wearing soiled underwear.'

'That girl's lucky, I don't know when I've pooed. And I bet she does care. She probably just doesn't like talking about her problem. I don't really like talking about it either.'

'Okay, we won't talk about it anymore,' says Carrie. She hands me back the iPad.

'Are you going to tell everyone?' I ask her.

'Of course not. I told you, I only teased you because I didn't really think you'd done it. I won't tell anyone, I promise.'

'Thanks,' I say, 'I don't want to be teased again like I was at my last school.'

'Tell you what,' says Carrie, 'I'll tell you my secret.'

I wonder what her secret will be. It may be something she's made up, like she's really the child of a film star or she has a million pounds in her piggy bank. But it turns out to be something very different.

'Some of the things I say at school aren't true,' she tells me. 'I haven't really been to Jupiter and the Prime Minister didn't really come to my birthday party.'

I don't know how to reply. I don't want to tell her that everyone knows she's lying when she says these things. She's not really telling me a secret at all, she's telling me what we all knew anyway.

But Carrie hasn't finished. She goes on, 'I do it because I don't know what to say when Miss Robbins asks us to tell the class what we've been doing over the weekend. Or when she wants us to write about an exciting day we've had. Mum and Dad don't take me out to exciting places. We don't go out at all very often. Mum says we haven't got enough money to go to lots of nice places. Dad doesn't make a lot of money at work. And he says it's hard with so many mouths to feed. I've got two brothers, you know, and now a baby sister as well. We can't go to the cinema because Mum says it would cost too much to buy five tickets and pay for a babysitter for Molly, my sister. And I've never been on a shopping trip to London and gone to all the big shops like Imogen has.'

'Oh Carrie,' I say, 'that's really hard on you, but you don't have to make up stories. People won't mind if your family aren't rich.'

'But I've never even had a birthday party,

Beth. Mum thinks if she lets me have one then she has to let my brothers have one as well. She says she can't afford the party food or the goodie bags. I don't go to friends' parties either because I won't be able to invite them back to my own party.'

'Tell you what,' I say, making a quick decision. 'you can come to my party on Saturday. It won't be a big party, just me and Ryan and my old friend Vicky and my little brother and a few cousins, but they'll be games and things. And my Dad makes a brilliant birthday cake. And I know I won't be able to come to your party because you're not having one and it doesn't matter.'

I watch as Carrie's eyes light up. 'Really? I can really come to your party?'

'Yes! Please come, Carrie, it'll be great to have another friend there.'

'Okay, I'll come. And you won't tell anyone my secret?'

'Never. And you promise you won't tell anyone mine?'

'Cross my heart and hope to die.'

Don't forget about Number 1!

> If you often put off going to the toilet to do a wee for a long time, you can damage your kidneys and bladder.

Listen to your bladder, even when you're busy

Chapter Nine
A LESSON LEARNED

It looks like everything is going to be all right. It's now Friday after school and I'm in my bedroom. Carrie hasn't told anyone about what I did in assembly on Wednesday. I haven't had any more accidents this week either. Great! Now I'm looking forward to being 9 tomorrow and my birthday party. You're invited to my party as well, of course. I think…oh, I'll have to talk to you later. Got to go to the toilet, got to do a poo. See you in a few minutes!

I'm back! Sorry I dashed off like that. But I know that when my body tells me I need a poo I must go to the toilet as soon as I can. Right at the start of this book I told you I put up my left hand to tell Miss Robbins I need to leave the room. It may be so I can change my pants, but I often do it so I can get to the toilet quickly. Miss Robbins doesn't mind, she knows what will happen if I ignore the need to poo. And so do I.

If it happens while I am out with Mum or Dad then I tell them right away and they find a toilet for me to use as quickly as they can. If we're in a shop which doesn't have toilets for customers then they ask if I can use the ones that the people who work there use. We even keep a travel potty in the car. Once or twice I've had to sit on it between the car doors on the side of the road. Not the best place to have a poo but much, much better than having an accident. Ryan's Mum has a travel potty in her car too for when she takes Ryan and me to different places, and she doesn't mind if I have to use it. She even has an app on her mobile phone that finds the nearest toilet when we're out. Ryan doesn't mind either if we have to stop what we're doing because I need a poo. Of course, I always take spare pants with me as well, but I don't have to use them much these days.

I wasn't always so quick to go to the toilet. I think I've already told you that I didn't like asking to go for a poo at day nursery. I could go for a wee by myself, but I didn't like asking a grown-up to take me for a poo, and then stay there while I did it and wipe my bum when I said I'd finished. It wasn't too bad when Miss Qureshi or Mr Francis took me to the toilet, because they were really nice. But I really didn't like it when Mrs Vernon took me, because she always told me I was old enough to wipe my own bottom. She also said the same thing to Vicky, and Vicky is two and a half months younger than me. I think Mrs Vernon just didn't like wiping kids' bums!

Then, when I had been at day nursery a few weeks, I found a way of avoiding using the toilet when I needed a poo. I just used to breathe in, clench my bottom and squeeze my legs together and the feeling went away. Then I'd carry on playing. Sometimes the feeling came back and I'd just do the same thing again.

It wasn't like when I needed a wee. If I ignored that feeling then it just kept getting worse, until I either went to the toilet or wee'd in my pants. I only wet myself once at day nursery, which taught me that I could not ignore my body when it told me I needed to wee. But I thought I could get away with not pooing. I never asked an adult to take me to do a poo at day nursery again.

I started using the same trick when we went out and I needed a poo. I didn't like pooing in public toilets so I just made the feeling go away. I told myself I would use the toilet when we were home again. Sometimes I did but found I couldn't go. And sometimes I forgot or just didn't bother trying. I didn't really like pooing in friends' homes either so I did the same thing there. Vicky once spotted me squeezing my knees together and breathing in. She asked me what I was doing and I told her 'stopping my poo-poo coming out.' She thought I was being really clever. I wasn't.

I started getting bad tummy aches and had a few accidents. But the dirty pants always came later and I didn't know it was because I had stopped myself pooing. So I carried on doing it. I thought the poo just disappeared when I held it in. I didn't feel the need to poo anymore, so the poo must have gone away, I told myself.

By the time I was 5 my body had stopped telling me a lot of the time when I needed to poo. If I did try to use the toilet it often hurt, so I stopped trying. I had more and more accidents and didn't even know when I was doing it. I had Sneaky Poo.

My doctor called what I was doing 'withholding.' He said a lot of children do it, stopping themselves from going to the toilet and keeping their poo inside their body. Some children really fight hard to stop themselves pooing. And some children do it so long that it becomes a habit and they do it without thinking about it. But he told me that stopping yourself from doing a poo is a very bad thing to do. And it often leads to Sneaky Poo.

I told the doctor how I thought I could make my poo disappear. He smiled and told me that a lot of children think this. But he said I couldn't make poo disappear by not using the toilet. It had to go somewhere, and if it didn't go in the toilet then it would go in my pants. And my body didn't care if I was at school, playing with friends, in a busy shop or on a lovely day out when it pushed the poo out and made me stinky and my pants messy.

So I've learnt my lesson. These days I never ignore what my body is telling me. And neither should you. If you feel you need to do a poo, always go to the toilet!

> I don't want the kids in my class holding in their poo.

> Nor do I, so I put up the poster on the next page in my classroom.

REMEMBER, EVERYBODY POOS!
(INCLUDING TEACHERS!)

If you need to poo, you know what to do!

Put up your hand and go to the loo!

It's COOL to POO at SCHOOL!

Chapter Ten
'HAPPY BIRTHDAY, BETH!'

'Happy Birthday, Beth!' says Carrie as she arrives at my party.

'Thanks, Carrie,' I say, 'and thanks for coming.' I give her a hug, then my Mum helps her to take her coat off.

Carrie hands me a little parcel. 'I couldn't afford to buy you a present so I made you this.'

I open it up. Inside is a bracelet made from old buttons and plastic beads. It looks great, Carrie is obviously very clever at making things. 'It's lovely,' I tell her. I put it on my wrist. It goes really well with my party dress.

Carrie is wearing normal clothes, but I don't mind at all. It's just so nice to have another friend and not have to worry about having an accident. I'm going round to play at her house on Tuesday and I'll meet her brothers and her baby sister. And my Mum wants to take Carrie, Ryan and me to the funfair next weekend. Carrie's really looking forward to that because she's never been to a fair before.

'We're going to eat first,' I tell Carrie, 'and have games afterwards. We'll start tea as soon as Ryan gets here. He's the only one who hasn't arrived yet. Come with me and I'll introduce you to Vicky and my cousins. Oh, and I suppose you'll have to meet my brother as well.'

Jack is actually being nice to me today. It may be because he thinks that it wouldn't be kind to be mean to me on my birthday. But I think it's more likely that he knows that he won't get a piece of my birthday cake if he's not on his best behaviour. No doubt tomorrow he'll be calling me 'smelly girly' again.

It's five minutes later and Ryan has arrived. I give him a big hug and he gives me my present. I open it up and find that it's the book that I've wanted to read for ages and ages. Well, I have been dropping hints to him about it for the last two months!

I show him the bracelet that Carrie has

made for me. 'It's great, isn't it?' I say. 'Carrie must be really clever to be able to make something like this. I'm going round her house on Tuesday so I'll ask her to show me how to do it.'

He looks at the bracelet an me. 'It's nice,' he says.

Okay, not the highest my present. Maybe I shouldn't have expected a boy to be too bothered about a piece of jewellery. But I think there might be another reason why he's not exactly excited about my present from Carrie. He's worried that I'm going to want to spend all my time with my new friend rather than him.

How could he think that? The boy who didn't complain when I stank out his Mum's car on the motorway. The boy who let me borrow his favourite *Batman* pants when I forgot to take my spare pants to his house (I was a bit scared to wear them, but he said it didn't matter if I had another accident and dirtied them, they could be washed.) The boy who saved up his pocket money to buy me some new *Frozen* pants after I had shared with him my worst memory of pooing myself in public while watching the lions. And the boy who closed his eyes, held his nose and let me do a poo in the toilet while he was in the bath on the morning after a sleepover, because he didn't want me to risk having an accident. (We had baths together when we first started having sleepovers, but we don't anymore! And no, Ryan didn't wee in the water like my brother did! Well only once, but he really needed to go and he did ask me before he did it!)

'Don't worry, Ryan,' I say to him, 'you're my best friend forever.' And then I do something I've never done before. I lean forward and kiss him on the cheek.

'Got you!' says a voice. We turn round together to see my Mum has taken a picture of me kissing Ryan on her mobile phone. 'This is going straight on my Facebook page.'

'Mum, don't put that Ryan is my boyfriend, will you?' I plead with her.

'Of course not. Best friends, right?'

'Right,' say Ryan and me together.

'Come on then, birthday girl and best friend,' says Mum, 'I think it's time for you to blow out the candles on your birthday cake, Beth. Then all you hungry children can get something to eat. Into the kitchen, both of you.'

We follow her into the kitchen where everyone else is waiting. My birthday cake is shaped like a big number 9 and, of course, has nine candles on it. My Dad is lighting the candles. When all nine candles have been lit he asks everyone to sing to me. I stand there smiling as everyone sings 'Happy Birthday to You.' When they have finished, Mum asks me to blow out the candles on my cake and make a wish.

I take a deep breath and blow. Four candles go out. I take another breath and blow again. Another two candles go out. I take the biggest breath of all and manage to blow out the last three candles. Everyone starts cheering and I smile.

I can't tell you what I wished for, because if I do that then it won't come true. But it's the same thing I wished for on my sixth birthday. And on my seventh. And on my eighth.

And one day soon it *will* come true.

Good Luck!

You can do it!

ABOUT THE AUTHOR

James Parkin's first books for children were the *Ghost Gang* series, which featured a group of friendly ghosts who help the children who have problems at Claire Rock Primary School. He wrote these three books while at university, drawing on several years experience of doing voluntary work in various local primary schools, day nurseries and playgroups with children of all ages from 0 to 11. He brought out revised editions of these books in 2012.

James had encopresis as a child and often soiled himself until he was 11. At the time, and for several years afterwards, he thought he was the only school aged child in the world who still pooed his pants. Years later he was surprised to find letters on the problem pages in newspapers and magazines from worried parents whose children often soiled themselves, including an 11 year old girl who frequently messed her pants and, like him, couldn't explain why she did it. With the arrival of the internet James discovered just how widespread a problem soiling was among children and teenagers.

As an adult he has tried to use his experiences to help today's children and their parents who are struggling with this embarrassing condition. He has published two blogs, where his honest and candid discussion of his childhood soiling has been appreciated by many parents.

In 2014 he wrote a book for older children who soil their pants, which he republished two years later in separate editions for boys and girls called *A Boy Like You* and *A Girl Like You*. Many children who have poo accidents, and their parents, have found these books very useful, and they have been endorsed by the children's continence charity ERIC. In 2020 he wrote and published *Help! I Poo My Pants* for boys and girls aged 5 to 8 who withhold their poo instead of going to the toilet and then mess their pants, which he hopes will prove equally useful to younger children and their parents.

He has also written *News from the Loos*, a book of short stories for all children aged 7 to 11, to try to raise awareness and understanding of children's toilet problems and encourage good bladder and bowel health at school and elsewhere. He hopes that it is also a fun read for kids!

James is single, lives in the UK and has a First Class BA (Hons) degree in Education Studies and History from De Montfort University.

The author's blogs about his soiling problems

For parents

childhoodsoiling.blogspot.co.uk

For children

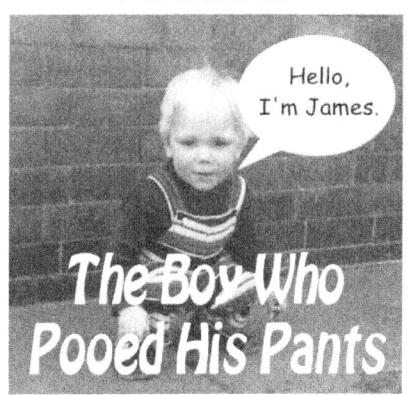

theboywhopooedhispants.blogspot.co.uk

FACEBOOK

There are several groups on Facebook for parents of children who soil. One of the largest groups, of which the author is a member and administrator, is called *HELP!!!! My Child Has Encopresis*. At the time of writing, this group had over 7,000 members across the globe.

The group is a great forum for posting ideas on what works and what doesn't for treating children's constipation and soiling problems, sharing success stories and letting off steam on bad days. No subject is TMI, and there is, naturally, much talk about poo, the toilet and soiled pants! Advice for dealing with schools and the medical profession is also regularly sought and offered, and matters which may be related to encopresis are also dealt with, such as wetting problems and behavioural issues.

For many parents simply being among others who are raising an encopretic child is a great support and comfort, as is the ability to discuss matters they feel they cannot talk about with their family and friends.

The author would like to thank the group for their support for these books, and their help in some of the phrasing for the American editions.

Other Facebook groups for parents set up by the author

Daytime Wetting in Children and Teens

Bedwetting in Children and Teens

Also available by the same author

Help! I Poo My Pants

AVAILABLE IN SEPARATE EDITIONS FOR BOYS AND GIRLS

A story for younger children who withhold their poo and soil their pants

Recommended age 5 to 8 years

For details please go to
www.bigredsock.com

Also available by the same author

Come and join us in the toilets!

NEWS from the LOOS

Stories from the School Toilets

"Hi, I'm Penny Spender, Librarian and School Toilets Reporter! Join me and the kids of Parktree Primary School as we tell you tales from the new Key Stage 2 unisex loos. Find amusing, sometimes embarrassing, stories in this fun book for all kids aged 7 to 11."

For details please go to
www.bigredsock.com

Also available by the same author

GHOST GANG

The New Ghost
Helen's Heartaches
Complicated Creatures

> Come and meet Claire Rock Primary School's friendly ghosts!

Recommended reading age 8 to 12 years

*Available in paperback
and for the Kindle and Kindle apps
from Amazon*

ERIC
The Children's Bowel and Bladder Charity

The UK based charity ERIC (Education and Resources for Improving Childhood Continence) is unique in focusing on all aspects of childhood toilet issues: potty training, bedwetting, daytime wetting, constipation and soiling.

Based in Bristol, ERIC offer a confidential helpline, training seminars for healthcare and other professionals, and an online shop, which sells, among other items, literature, bedwetting alarms, daytime pants and bedding protection.

Recent campaigns ERIC has run include *The Right to Go*, to highlight every child's right to good care for a continence problem at school and access to safe and hygienic school toilets at all times, and *Let's Talk About Poo*, to raise awareness of children's poo problems.

ERIC's website (www.eric.org.uk) is packed with information on all aspects of children's toileting, including soiling problems. There is also a website to encourage healthy bowels in children, which includes the Let's Talk About Poo Game: letstalkaboutpoo.eric.org.uk

You can contact ERIC in the following ways:

Telephone:
Helpline and information:
> 0845 370 8008 (within the UK only)
> *Telephone charges apply, please check website for current rates.*

Main switchboard:
> 0117 960 3060 (within the UK)
> +44 117 960 3060 (from outside the UK)

Postal address:
ERIC
36 Old School House
Britannia Road
Kingswood
BRISTOL
BS15 8DB
United Kingdom

ERIC is a small charity working in an unglamorous area and reliant on donations. Please consider donating money or fundraising for ERIC so that it can continue its vital work for children and families. ERIC receives all profits from sales of the author's books which are sold through their online shop.

ERIC is a Registered Charity (no 1002424) and a Company Limited by Guarantee (no 2580579) registered in England and Wales.